Where Is the Exit?

Practicing the GZ Sound

Lee Young

T0019168

Can you find the exit?
Examine each exit you see.

This is an exit on a plane.

This is an exit on a train.

This is an exit at the store.

This is an exit at a school.

Even roads have exits.
This is an exit sign.

Some exits do not have signs
to examine.

Can you think of an example?

This door is the exit
for a house.

This door is the exit
for a car.

Do other exits exist?